Reading
Genesis
&
Modern
Science:
A Study
Guide

Reading Genesis & Modern Science: A Study Guide

Frank & David DeHaan

credo
house publishers

Contents

Acknowledgments

We thank the following people for taking time to read our manuscript and for their many helpful comments and suggestions: Dan Beerens, Micah Bruxvoort, Drew Chamberlin, Gregg Davidson, Jane De Haan, Judy Hardy, Martin Huizinga, Randy Isaac, Marilou Kratzenstein, George Kroeze, Sandy Swartzentruber, and Steve Timmerman.

Special thanks to Audrey De Haan, who imagined and created the cartoons for each lesson and designed the cover.

I need to single out the adult Sunday school class of Bethel Church, Sun Valley, California, for their enthusiastic response to the discussions I led on some of the book's topics. That encouragement pushed us to seek a broader audience.

1

Introduction

Among issues that divide Christians today, questions about the age of the Earth and the universe are particularly troubling.

All Christians believe that the Bible is the inspired Word of God. As Protestant Reformers wrote in the Westminster Confession in 1646, the Bible is "to be the rule of faith and life." Some Christians, based on the description in the first chapter of Genesis, assert that the creation of the Earth literally took place in the span of six 24-hour days just over 6000 years ago. They feel as though any other view is ignoring the biblical text. Other Christians argue that it is a misuse of the Bible to attempt to use it to answer scientific questions, such as How old is the Earth? This second group prefers to acknowledge the validity of scientific evidence on this topic. Unfortunately, these two groups of Christians often look down on each other for being either, on the one hand, simplistic and naive or, on the other, unorthodox and compromising. Often it is easier, and less painful, to try to avoid the topic altogether. Does it really matter what Christians believe about the age of the Earth?

We think it does matter. The first approach often leads to the rejection of entire fields of modern science, including geology, cosmology, and evolutionary biology, along with bits of chemistry and much of genetics. And it isn't just about the distant past. Once you've begun to reject scientific truth that seems inconvenient, you may end up without the benefits of science at all as you decide how to approach pressing issues now and how to prepare for them in the future. The second approach has its own hazards that, for followers of Christ, are even more serious. If you start to reject parts of the Bible that seem inconvenient to you, you will likely end up with an anemic, ineffective, or misdirected faith.

Can we help each other avoid these negative outcomes? If the saying "All truth is God's truth" is valid, Christians should have little to fear from the progress of science. And if the Bible is indeed the inspired Word of God, we need to pay attention to all of it, being careful to the best of our knowledge and ability to interpret it correctly. Can we take both science and the Bible seriously, or do we have to ignore all or part of either one at the expense of the other? Can we regard each correctly and appropriately, while remaining consistent?

To see the challenge, let's look at a few numbers:

Age of the Earth:
~4,500,000,000 YEARS or 6,000–7,000 YEARS?

Age of the Universe:
~14,000,000,000 YEARS or 6,000–7,000 YEARS?

On the left you have the scientific community's current estimates of the age of the age of the Earth and the universe. On the right are the corresponding values from the Creation Research Society, taken from adding up numbers from the genealogies in the book of Genesis and elsewhere in the Bible. Believers who agree with one set of estimates or the other are often differentiated as "old Earth" Christians or "young Earth " Christians, respectively. As you can see by the disparity in the numbers, the two sets of estimates couldn't be further apart. Clearly, they can't both be right!

4

This study aims to clarify the reasoning behind the two positions in the hope that some productive discussion can take place. As scientists and Christians, we hope to encourage you to be open to the scientific evidence coming from God's revelation in nature, without discounting God's special revelation in the Bible.

Our goals in this study are for you to:

1. Appreciate the strength of the scientific evidence for an old Earth and universe.
2. Critique from a scientific perspective the approach/ methods used to reach a "young Earth" conclusion.
3. Utilize alternate ways to understand early Genesis chapters, especially Genesis 1.
4. Express why this really matters to a Christian today.

Then, looking to the future, we'd like to help you to:

5. Understand the causes, magnitude, and seriousness of global climate change.
6. Consider what you can do now to take better care of God's Earth.

The Age of the Earth: Continental Drift

For centuries geographers have noticed how—if you could move them—the east coast of South America and the west coast of Africa could fit together like puzzle pieces (Figure 1). In 1912 Alfred Wegener proposed a *Theory of Continental Drift* that he based partly on this puzzle-like fit between South America and Africa. His idea was that at one time these continents were joined but that they have since drifted apart. His theory was supported not just by the shape of the coastlines but also by identical plant and animal fossils, as well as by rock belts found at the "matching" points along the coastlines of South America and Africa. Since there is no way these fossils and rocks could have been transported across an ocean by a natural process, Wegener reasoned that some 200 million years ago—based on the age of the fossils—South America and Africa must have been joined together into one continent. He called this supercontinent Pangaea (Figure 2).

Fig 1. In 1858 geographer Antonio Snider-Pellegrini made these two maps showing his version of how the American and African continents may once have fit together, then later separated. Left: The formerly joined continents before (*avant*) their separation. Right: The continents after (*aprés*) the separation. (Reproductions of the original maps courtesy of University of California, Berkeley.)

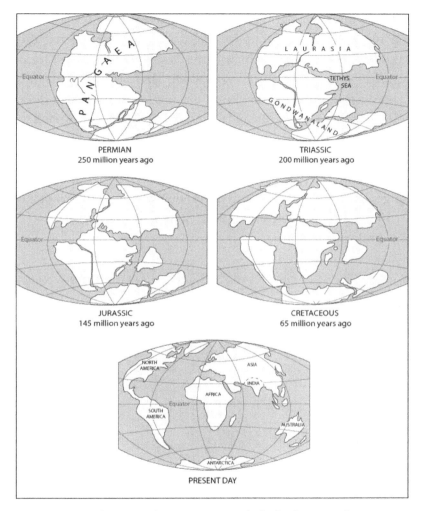

Fig 2. According to the continental drift theory, the super-continent Pangaea began to break up about 200–225 million years ago, eventually fragmenting into the continents as we know them today. (U. S. Geological Survey)

This idea that Africa and South America have been slowly moving apart gained support when geologists discovered the Middle-Atlantic Ridge, which is the "seam" at which two rigid plates are moving away from each other. This causes new magma from deep in the Earth to rise to the surface of the ocean floor and generate the ridge. It can be seen in Figure 3 as the black line separating the South American plate from the African plate, with two–headed arrows indicating the plates pulling apart from each other. In other regions plates collide head-on to create mountain ranges like the Himalayas and the Andes, while in California the Pacific and North American plates slide past each other on the San Andreas fault line.

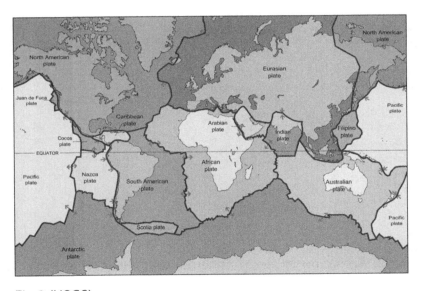

Fig 3 (USGS)

GPS can detect motions along faults today, and along the Middle Atlantic Ridge the plates are moving apart at a speed of 2.5–5 cm/year. Given that Rio de Janeiro, Brazil, South America, and

Luanda, Angola, Africa are separated by 3,856 miles, if the plate movement has been at a constant rate this suggests that the two continents separated approximately 125 to 250 million years ago.

Other evidence also suggests long-term drifts. Geologists have measured magnetic variations along the ocean floor in strips parallel to the mid-ocean ridge. As the magma solidifies when it reaches the cooler ocean floor, the direction of magnetization of minerals with magnetic elements (e.g., iron) is "frozen" and therefore reflects the Earth's magnetic field at that time, as shown in Figure 4.

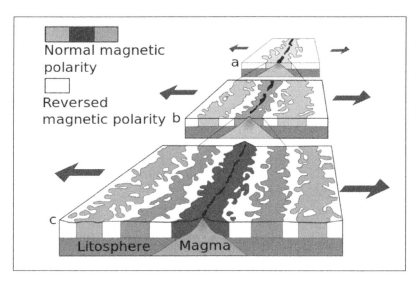

Fig 4 USGS

From other data we know that the Earth's dipole moment (the strength and direction of its magnetic field) continues to change, but very gradually (Figures 5 and 6). When mid-19th-century measurements showed that the Earth's dipole moment was decreasing, some jumped to the conclusion that this decrease could be smoothly extrapolated into the past. Estimating the maximum possible dipole moment, and using an exponential decay function, they suggested that this trend provided scientific evidence that the Earth is less than 10,000 years old. However, later analysis of archaeological materials (and current modeling, Figure 5) showed that the Earth's dipole moment actually peaked around the year 1700 and was rising for many centuries before that. The sea floor measurements suggest that Earth's dipole moment has varied over long time periods in a random pattern and has reversed itself many times.

In summary, continental drift or plate tectonics are not useful to date the age of the planet but show plainly that processes we can observe today have been ongoing for much longer than 6,000–7,000 years.

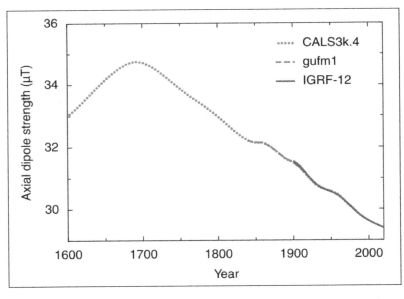

Fig 5: Strength of Earth's dipole moment since 1600 according to three different models. Models are validated by comparison to measurements (1835–present) and to archaeological

materials. From Wikimedia Commons, produced by Cavit [CC BY 4.0 (http://creativecommons.org/licenses/by/4.0)].[3]

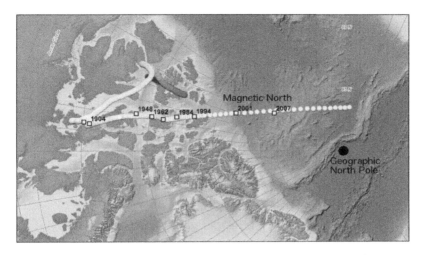

Fig 6: Changing position of Earth's geomagnetic north pole (the direction of the magnetic field) from 1590–2020, showing its movement across the Canadian Arctic and into the Arctic Ocean. The geographic north pole is marked with a black circle. Greenland is at the bottom center of map. From NOAA's National Centers for Environmental Information.[4]

Questions for Lesson One

1. Is the tectonic plate map, Figure 3, an indicator of Earth's major earthquake fault lines? Note: These questions and our answers and comments appear in a section immediately following Notes. See Contents.

2. If new solidified magma continues to be formed along the Middle Atlantic Ridge—i.e., the Americas are moving away from Europe and Africa—why is the Earth not increasing in size?

3. Are earthquakes the result of the fall of humanity (Genesis 3)? In other words, is it likely that earthquakes began with Adam?

4. Is there such a thing as a human-caused earthquake?

5. What is a tsunami? Are these a product of the fall?

The Age of the Earth: Radioactive Decay

Dating rocks.

One type of evidence for the age of the Earth comes from measurements of different types of atoms. Since the authors of this guide are both chemists, we'll go into some detail on this. We'd like to help you understand this evidence, but to do that we'll need to dig into some background information so it will make more sense. If you feel yourself getting bogged down in the scientific details in the next two "background information" sections, you should feel free to skip to the following section, titled "**How does radioactive decay allow us to determine how old things are?**"

Background Information: Isotopes

Atoms, the stuff out of which everything is made, can be distinguished into almost 110 different types, called "elements." But many elements, even when 100% pure, can be further subdivided by mass into different groups called "isotopes." Take a look at the list of isotopes of lead (Pb) and uranium (U) shown below.[5] Lead exists as 19 different isotopes, and uranium exists as 14 isotopes, so the list is rather long. Here's how to read the list of isotopes. To the lower left of each element symbol ("Pb" or "U") is the isotope's number of protons (positively charged particles within the nucleus). To the upper right of each element symbol is the mass number—the total weight of the nucleus. As you can see, all isotopes of a given element have the same number of protons—82 for lead and 92 for uranium. However, each lead isotope contains a different number of neutrons (non-charged particles within the nucleus). The first isotope of lead in the list has 112 neutrons and 82 protons, which add up to 194, the mass number, so it gets listed as Pb^{194} or "lead-194." This is the lightest known lead isotope. Other Pb isotopes weigh more because of extra neutrons in their nuclei. (We'll get to the other stuff shown on this list a bit later.)

ISOTOPES OF LEAD (Pb) AND URANIUM (U)[5]

Isotope	Percent Abundance	Exact Mass	Half-Life	Decay Mode
$_{82}Pb^{194}$			11 m	EC
$_{82}Pb^{195}$			17 m	EC
$_{82}Pb^{196}$			37 m	EC
$_{82}Pb^{198}$			2.4 hr	EC
$_{82}Pb^{199}$			1.2 m	EC
$_{82}Pb^{200}$			21.5 hr	EC
$_{82}Pb^{201}$			9.5 hr	EC
$_{82}Pb^{202}$		201.9722	3×10^5 yr	EC
$_{82}Pb^{203}$		202.97321	52 hr	EC
$_{82}Pb^{204}$	1.48	203.97307	Stable	
$_{82}Pb^{205}$		204.97452	3×10^7 yr	EC
$_{82}Pb^{206}$	23.6	205.97446	Stable	
$_{82}Pb^{207}$	22.6	206.97590	Stable	
$_{82}Pb^{208}$	52.3	207.97664	Stable	
$_{82}Pb^{209}$		208.98111	3.3 hr	β^-
$_{82}Pb^{210}$		209.98418	22 yr	β^-
$_{82}Pb^{211}$		210.98880	36.1 m	β^-
$_{82}Pb^{212}$		211.99190	10.6 hr	β^-
$_{82}Pb^{214}$		213.9998	26.8 m	β^-
$_{92}U^{227}$		227.0309	1.3 m	α
$_{92}U^{228}$		228.03128	9.3 m	α
$_{92}U^{229}$		229.0332	58 m	EC

Isotope	Percent Abundance	Exact Mass	Half-Life	Decay Mode
$_{92}U^{230}$		230.03393	21 d	α
$_{92}U^{231}$		231.0363	4.3 d	EC
$_{92}U^{232}$		232.03717	74 yr	α
$_{92}U^{233}$		233.03950	1.62×10^5 yr	α
$_{92}U^{234}$	0.0056	234.0409	2.48×10^5 yr	α
$_{92}U^{235}$	0.7205	235.04393	7.13×10^8 yr	α
$_{92}U^{236}$		236.04573	2.4×10^7 yr	α
$_{92}U^{237}$		237.04858	6.75 d	β⁻
$_{92}U^{238}$	99.274	238.0508	4.51×10^9 yr	α
$_{92}U^{239}$		239.0543	23.5 m	β⁻
$_{92}U^{240}$		240.05670	14 h	β⁻

Background Information: Radioactive Decay

Neutrons change more than just the weight of an atom, however. If you look in the "half-life" column of the list, you will also notice that only Pb^{204}, Pb^{206}, Pb^{207}, and Pb^{208} are stable, meaning that these atoms can last forever. All other Pb isotopes and all uranium isotopes have unstable nuclei—nuclei that break down at some point. They are "radioactive."

The breakdown of a nucleus is known as radioactive decay, and this breakdown, because it changes the number of protons, changes an atom of one element into an atom of another. How quickly a nucleus will break down depends on the stability of the nucleus, which in turn depends on the number of neutrons.

An atom's nucleus will be unstable if it has too few *or* too many neutrons! As seen in Figure 7—a graph of the number of neutrons (N) vs. the number of protons (Z) in all 256 known stable isotopes—the points all fall in a diagonal stripe known as the *band of stability*. Looking more closely at the left side of the graph, you can see that the numbers of protons and neutrons must be nearly the same in order for smaller atoms to be stable. This relationship is shown as a dashed diagonal line labeled "N/Z = 1." Larger atoms need extra neutrons in order to be stable—the "magic number" appears to be about N/Z = 1.5, or 1.5 neutrons for each proton in the nucleus. This is shown as the higher, solid line in Figure 7.

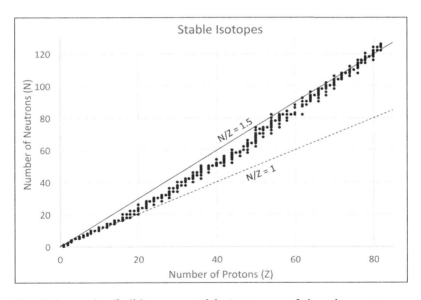

Fig 7: A graph of all known stable isotopes of the elements, according to the number of neutrons (N) and protons (Z) each contains.[6]

As an example of an atom with an unstable nucleus, let's look at $_6C^{14}$, called carbon 14. $_6C^{14}$ is formed in the upper atmosphere when a regular nitrogen atom captures a neutron streaming in from the sun. Written as a nuclear reaction, the process looks like this:

$$_7N^{14} + _0n^1 \rightarrow _6C^{14} + _1H^1$$

In this reaction $_0n^1$ is the neutron and $_1H^1$ is a proton, which is the same thing as a hydrogen atom nucleus, and so is given the symbol "H." (In nuclear reactions, an electron is shown only when it gets created or destroyed in the nucleus, not when it is just whizzing around nearby in its usual way.) Note that N/Z = 1 for $_7N^{14}$ (7 protons and 7 neutrons), and it is perfectly stable, while $_6C^{14}$ has a N/Z ratio of 14/6. This puts $_6C^{14}$ above the band of stability in Figure 1—it has too many neutrons! Therefore, at some point it will undergo radioactive decay in such a way that will drop its N/Z ratio back toward 1. Written out, this radioactive decay looks like this:

$$_6C^{14} \rightarrow _7N^{14} + _{-1}e^0$$

In essence, a neutron inside the $_6C^{14}$ nucleus disintegrates into a proton and an electron. The proton remains in the nucleus, which changes the identity of the atom to nitrogen (since it now has seven protons instead of six). The electron, on the other hand, comes flying out of the nucleus at a high speed. This is known as a beta particle. The radioactive elements that decay in this way are labeled in the isotope list with a beta symbol (β) under "decay mode."

This decay may not happen right away. In fact, it is impossible to predict when an individual carbon-14 atom will decay.

20

However, the decay of large numbers of radioactive atoms is predictable using statistics. Since just a milligram of carbon-14 contains 4 x 10^{19} atoms—that's "4" followed by 19 zeros!!—it is hard to end up with a situation in which you are *not* dealing with large numbers of atoms. So we can generalize that radioactive materials (large groups of atoms) always follow the statistical decay law, which is illustrated in Figure 8.

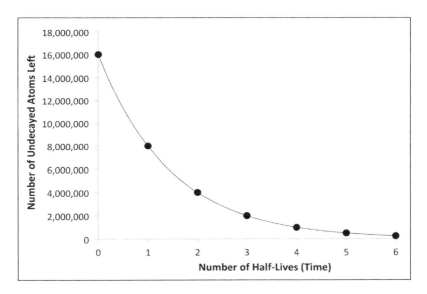

Fig 8: Decay curve for radioactive isotopes

The only difference between one radioactive isotope and another, in terms of how they follow the statistical decay law, is the length of time represented by a "half-life." If you gathered 16 million C^{14} atoms together in a container that never leaked, half of them would still be there 5,715 years later, while the other half would have decayed during that period into nitrogen-14 atoms. Another way of saying this is that carbon-14 has a half-life represented as $t_{1/2}$

of 5,715 years. After another 5,715 years have gone by, half of the remaining carbon-14 atoms would have decayed to nitrogen-14, leaving only a quarter of the original carbon-14 atoms in the container. At this point two half-lives would have gone by. It turns out that we can accurately predict how many carbon-14 atoms will be in the container for many half-lives, until the number gets so small that statistics are no longer useful.

Scientists have measured the length of a half-life for many different isotopes. If you take a second look at the half-lives column in our list of lead and uranium isotopes, you will see that the half-life for lead-199 is only 1.2 minutes, meaning that you'd get all the way across Figure 2 in just over 7 minutes. On the other hand, some of the uranium isotopes have extremely long half-lives—if it weren't for the energy of radioactive decay coming from uranium samples, people would have assumed they were stable elements, since they change so slowly!

How does radioactive decay allow us to determine how old things are?

Let's start with *carbon dating*. We humans get energy from our food when we digest sugars and other molecules, combining them with the oxygen we breathe to produce carbon dioxide and water. We can express this through the chemical "equation"

$$[CH_2O] + O_2 \rightarrow CO_2 + H_2O$$

where the square brackets mean "lots of these atoms combined in various ways."

Fortunately (and we can thank God for this!), plants run this reaction in reverse, converting our waste products back into food and oxygen and pulling CO_2 out of the atmosphere. The vast majority of this carbon getting converted back and forth is C^{12}. But a little bit of C^{14} is constantly being produced high in the atmosphere, as described earlier, so that living plants take up only a tiny percentage of it into their stems and leaves as they grow. Humans and animals absorb these carbon-14 atoms as they eat. Because we're constantly absorbing a very small amount of these carbon-14 atoms in our diet, and these atoms are decaying with a 5,715-year half-life, these processes balance each other out and the fraction of carbon-14 in our bodies becomes constant. As a result, as long as we (and plants and animals) are alive, we contain within ourselves a very small but constant fraction of carbon-14. However, when death occurs, the uptake process— eating or growing—stops. The C^{14} atoms are not replenished, so their numbers drop as they decay with a half-life of 5,715 years.

This decline in the fraction of C^{14} atoms upon death can be used to date artifacts. Let's say archaeologists find a small fragment of rope as they dig through the remains of an ancient village. Measurements of the carbon isotopes in the rope show that the C^{14} fraction is only 1/4 of that of living plants. Since 1/4 = (1/2)(1/2), the archaeologists then know that the rope was made from plant material that was last alive two C^{14} half-lives ago. Since the carbon-14 half-life is always 5,715 years, they will multiply:

2 (5715 years) = 11,430 years.

Their conclusion: the rope was made from plants that died approximately 11,430 years ago.

This carbon dating process is used to determine the age of hair, wood, leather, food, or any other formerly living material up to about 50,000 years old. This makes carbon dating great for studying the archaeological remains of ancient human societies. For artifacts that are much older than 50,000 years, there is too little C^{14} left to make a good measurement. The existence of many such artifacts that contain essentially no carbon-14, and are therefore too old for carbon dating, is certainly a challenge to the "young Earth" idea that the Earth is only 6,000–7,000 years old. But carbon dating cannot tell us much beyond that about the age of the Earth. To "date" the Earth, we'll need to turn to other isotopes with much longer half-lives.

Dating Rocks

Let's take a third look at the lead and uranium isotopes list. But first, it is important to note that the radioactive decay of U^{238} produces Pb^{206} by the multi-step process summarized in Figure 9. At each step in the process, the half-life for the radioactive decay is shown, along with the symbols α, β, and γ that refer to the type of decay. If you'd like to understand these different types of radioactive decay, you can read the following background information section. However, an understanding of these processes is not necessary for our larger purpose of estimating the age of the Earth from isotopic ratios. The important point in Figure 9 is that the longest half-life in the entire process is, by far, the first step. This means that the amount of lead-206 produced is controlled by the rate of the first step, which is the radioactive decay of U^{238}.

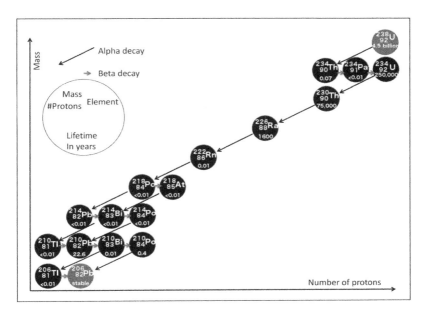

Fig 9: Radioactive decay pathway by which uranium-238 eventually produces lead-206.

Background Info: Types of Radioactive Decay

- Alpha (α) decay is the expulsion of a helium nucleus $_2He^4$, which consists of 2 protons and 2 neutrons and is called an alpha particle. Alpha decay is common among nuclei with more than 83 protons, since they are to the right of the band of stability in Figure 7. For example,

$$_{92}U^{238} \rightarrow {}_{90}Th^{234} + {}_2He^4$$

- Beta (β) decay is the expulsion of a high-energy electron (called a beta particle) from the nucleus. We already saw that carbon-14 does this:

$$_6C^{14} \rightarrow _7N^{14} + _{-1}e^0$$

The radioactive breakdown of thorium-234 is another example of beta decay:

$$_{90}Th^{234} \rightarrow _{91}Pa^{234} + _{-1}e^0$$

- Gamma (γ) decay is the release of high-energy radiation that often accompanies alpha or beta decay.
- EC, an abbreviation seen in the isotope list but not in Figure 9, stands for "electron capture." It is the capture of an inner shell electron by the nucleus, which results in a proton converting to a neutron:

$$_1p^1 + _{-1}e^0 \rightarrow _0n^1$$

Thus N/Z is increased. This process is likely when N/Z is *below* the band of stability (Figure 7).

Given that Pb^{206} can be produced only by U^{238} decay, let's now look at how geologists use this fact to date the age of rocks. As with carbon dating, we need to know something about isotopic ratios, both at present and when something was first formed. How does this work with rocks? Let's start with granite, which typically contains minerals known as zircon and feldspar:

Mineral	Chemical Formula	Name
zircon	$ZrSiO_4$	zirconium silicate (plus impurities)
feldspar		aluminum silicate, plus K, Na, Ca, or Ba and other impurities, but *not* U

We also need to mention the size of some of these atoms. The radius of each atom is listed below, in Angstroms. (An Angstrom is 0.1 billionth of a meter.)

Atomic radius: **Zr ~ 1.45 Angstroms**

U ~ 1.42 Angstroms

Al ~ 1.18 Angstroms

Note the similar sizes of Zr and U atoms. Because of this similarity, small amounts of uranium are found in zircons at some of the locations usually occupied by a zirconium atom. On the other hand, the mineral feldspar does not contain uranium, since uranium atoms are 20% larger than aluminum atoms. This means that uranium atoms would not fit in the places occupied by aluminum atoms. When granite is formed (crystallized from molten material), both zircons and feldspar should have the same ratio of Pb^{206}/Pb^{204} impurities, since these lead isotope atoms would be coming from the same molten material. After the granite is formed, as the rock ages the multi-step decay process $U^{238} \rightarrow Pb^{206}$ takes place in zircon, because of the small amount of U^{238} that it contains, and the Pb^{206}/Pb^{204} ratio slowly increases. Since there is no U^{238} in feldspar, however, the ratio does not change since no Pb^{206} is being produced. The difference in these ratios allows one to calculate the amount of U^{238} that has been transformed into Pb^{206} by radioactive decay. If the amount of undecayed U^{238} still present is also measured, this allows us to determine how many half-lives of U^{238} decay have gone by since the granite was first formed, and then we have a good estimate of the age of the rock.

For example, a small zircon that was recently found in western Australia was dated via the $U^{238} \rightarrow Pb^{206}$ method. Just under half of its U^{238} had decayed into Pb^{206}, which means that nearly one U^{238} half-life (4.4 billion years) had passed since the zircon crystallized. (The half-life of U^{238} is 4.51 billion years.) There are other radiometric dating methods that give the same result, such as potassium → argon and rubidium → strontium, as well as other uranium–thorium–lead isotope pathways (besides U^{238} → Pb^{206}, described above).[7] Many rocks have been dated, but none have been found that are more than 4.4 billion years old. This suggests to geologists that the Earth's crust must have cooled enough to become solid 4.4 billion years ago, and hence that the Earth must be at least this old.

Questions for Lesson Two

1. If one atom has 80 protons and another has 81 protons, are these different elements or different isotopes?

2. Despite the essential role of trees/forests in removing atmospheric CO_2, what are some factors responsible for continued deforestation in various parts of the Earth?

3. If you were a landholder in Mexico, would clear-cutting your forest and planting avocado trees constitute an effective response to the current huge demand emanating from China for that fruit? Why or why not?

4. Why is the age of the oldest rock not synonymous with the age of the Earth?

5. Why do this book's authors suggest 50,000 years as a practical limit to C-14 dating?

6. For those with an algebra/high school chemistry background, note that Figure 8 can also be expressed in straight line form. Since radioactive decay is a first-order process, i.e., depends only on the number of radioactive atoms present, it follows the equation

$$\frac{-dN}{dt} = \text{Rate of decay} = kN$$

where k is the first-order rate constant and N is the number of radioactive atoms. Using calculus, this equation becomes

$$\frac{-kt}{2.3} = \log \frac{N_t}{N_0} \qquad (1)$$

where t is the time span of the decay, N_0 the original number of radioactive atoms at t = 0, and N_t the number remaining at the end of the time interval. It follows that

$$\text{when } t = t_{1/2}, N_t = N_0 / 2$$
$$\text{and thus}$$
$$k = 0.693 / t_{1/2} \qquad (2)$$

Problem: If a rock contains 0.130 mg of Pb-206 for every 1.0 mg of U-238, how old is the rock? The half-life of U-238 is 4.51×10^9 years. What assumption must you make?

Answer: 9×10^8 years (see the working out of the solution on page 77).

7. For those interested in science, predict the mode of decay of $_{78}Pt^{186}$. The Periodic Table records the atomic weight of platinum as 195.08, which is a weighted average of six stable isotopes.

The Age of the Universe: The Big Bang Theory

Thanks to the work of Edwin Hubble and the telescope named after him, we now know that the universe is expanding in all directions. In fact, each galaxy's velocity is proportional to its distance from us. In other words, galaxies that are twice as far from us move twice as fast. Thus, each galaxy took the same amount of time to move to its current position from its starting position. And when we reverse the process with computers, we find that there is *one* point in space from which all galaxies are traveling away. This calculated starting point/beginning moment has become known as the Big Bang. Furthermore, if one does the calculations to determine when any two galaxies were in the same place at the same time, one finds the number to be approximately fifteen billion years. This is, therefore, the apparent age of the universe.

While a giant explosion followed by fifteen billion years of expansion sounds like a different creation story from the one in Genesis 1, there are some key similarities. The Big Bang contradicts the notion once held by most scientists that the universe had no beginning—that "it was just there." Scientific evidence now shows that the universe did in fact have a beginning, starting from nothing (or at least an empirically unknowable state)! This naturally causes people to wonder who or what started the universe, and for what purpose. Science has no way of answering such questions. Fortunately, the main point of Genesis 1 is to provide answers to "who" and "why" questions about our own existence and that of our surroundings.

When Christians decide not to accept the evidence of an ancient universe and the Big Bang, they are throwing away one of the strongest scientific arguments for believing in a Creator God. To express this in other words, the Big Bang Theory has forced many scientists and others to seriously consider the existence of God, along with other, related questions, such as whether he is knowable, personable, loving, etc.

Questions for Lesson Three

1. When did God create the universe?

2. How did God create the universe?

3. What did ancient/biblical peoples fear?
   Read Job 3:8

   Job 7:12

   Psalm 148:7

   Isaiah 27:1

   Isaiah 30:7

   Isaiah 51:9

4. How did ancient/biblical people view the Earth?
    Read Genesis 7:11

    Psalm 24:1–2

    Psalm 78:23

    Psalm 104:5

    Psalm 148:4

    Proverbs 8:27–28

    Isaiah 24:18b

    Isaiah 40:22

5. Where did God dwell?
    Read Psalm 104:3

    Amos 9:6

6. Were the days of creation 24-hour days as we know them?

7. Does God speak through creation, or only through the Bible?
    Read Psalm 19:1

    Psalm 111:2

    Psalm 145

    Psalm 147

    Psalm 148

    Colossians 1:15–17

Where Does the Idea of a Young Earth and Universe Come From?

In 1658 James Ussher, Archbishop of Armagh, in his *Annals of the World* stated that the Earth and the universe came into being in 4004 B.C. This was based on his literal interpretation of the Genesis genealogies and chronologies in Scripture. He was not alone; others, including Johannes Kepler and Sir Isaac Newton, proposed similar dates. It is likely that before this time the question of the exact age of the universe was not considered very important.

As Ralph D. Winter stated,[11] "Beginning seriously in 1810 Christian believers (and even Oxford professors) began to dig up huge bones in England which did not represent any then-existing creatures. In the next 100 years Christians by and large accepted the antiquity of such fossils. The Schofield Bible made allowance for an 'old earth'. The 'fundamental' books in the 1910s and 20s made allowance." Already in 1890 scholars such as Princeton professor William Henry Green wrote, "We conclude that the Scriptures furnish no data prior to the life of Abraham; and that the Mosaic records do not fix and were not intended to fix the precise date either of the Flood or the creation of the world."[12] Dr. Winter goes on to write, "But today, especially throughout the homeschool movement, an originally Seventh-Day Adventist theory of a flash creation of a young earth that only looked old has taken root and means many youth are unprepared to confront later on what are widely understood as facts."[11]

One of the major proponents of a 6,000-year-old Earth has been the Creation Research Society (founded in 1963), along with the Institute for Creation Research, who continue to promote their views on Christian radio and television stations and go so far as to push for their inclusion in public school curricula. Both Arkansas and Louisiana passed laws mandating such coverage; both laws were struck down by the courts.

The current situation is clearly described by Christian geologists Davis Young and Ralph Stearley:

> Despite the facts that young-Earth creationism has become considerably more sophisticated and that some of its proponents are much more geologically knowledgeable than were earlier advocates like Price

and Morris, the claims advanced in favor of a young earth or of Flood geology remain unacceptable to the scientific community. Thus their claims should also be unacceptable within the church, which, of all places, ought to be committed to truth and reality— for the simple reason that the young-Earth creationist claims lack scientific credibility. They neither discredit evidence for an old Earth nor compel acceptance of a young Earth or a global Flood.

A factor contributing to the remarkably widespread acceptance of young-Earth creationism since the nineteenth century is the strong link geology has acquired with the theory of biological evolution by natural selection, extending not only to lower animals and plants but to the human race as well. The scientific, strictly biological conception of evolution, unfortunately, has on occasion been transformed into an antireligious and anti-Christian philosophy by scientists and philosophers who are committed to lean toward materialism. The materialistic philosophies of these writers take human beings out of the realm of creatures who are accountable to a creator God and place them in a realm where they are subject only to blind, mechanical forces and inherited instincts. As a result of such polarizations, the scientific theory of biological development has become so closely identified with a materialistic worldview in the minds of many Christians, including young-earth creationists, that they throw out the baby with the bath water, calling not merely for the repudiation of materialism but also for the rejection of evolution as a legitimate scientific theory.

Without question, any purely materialistic philosophy is hostile to Christianity and ought to be opposed by Christians. Christians should not, however, attempt to disprove a materialistic evolutionary theory by discrediting the antiquity of the Earth. *Evolutionary materialism and the antiquity of the Earth are two distinct issues.* If the vast antiquity of the Earth is amply demonstrated, one must still evaluate the data and theory of evolution on their own *scientific* merits.

To summarize, in the face of the facts that the scientific community was virtually unanimous in accepting the vast antiquity of the Earth throughout the twentieth century right up to the present, and that geologic (and astronomical) evidence for such antiquity has continued to accumulate, significant segments of the Christian church have regressed by welcoming scientifically discredited ideas that include Flood geology and a very young Earth. For whatever reasons, acceptance of scientific findings prevails among academic theologians and the vast majority of Christian geologists, whereas acceptance of young-Earth creationism, anti-evolutionism and "Flood geology" prevails among pastors and lay Christians. Moreover, an astonishing number of Christians in the sciences other than geology and astronomy, along with numerous Christian physicians and engineers, are quite enthusiastic in their support of these discredited theories.

This state of affairs, in our judgment, reflects lack of appropriate geologic knowledge coupled with existence of tendencies to read Scripture in overly literalistic ways that fail to take into account the ancient Near Eastern cultural background of much of Scripture and the primary pedagogical concern of the Bible.[13]

Questions for Lesson Four

1. What is "flood geology"?

2. Why was Ussher's 1658 estimate of the age of the universe generally accepted for 150 years?

3. The scientific evidence in support of an ancient Earth and universe slowly accumulates, becoming stronger with each passing year. According to Gallup polls, 65–70% of weekly church-going Christians believe that God created humans in their present form within the last 10,000 years, and this percentage has held steady for at least 35 years. Why do you think this is so?

4. Many assume that science and religion have always disagreed. Is this accurate?

5. Why do some scientists push the idea that given the immensity of the universe humankind is insignificant? John Ortberg quotes astronomer Carl Sagan, who wrote that the Earth is "an insignificant planet of a humdrum star lost in a galaxy tucked away in some forgotten corner of a universe in which there are far more galaxies than people." Sagan also said, when introducing his TV program titled *The Cosmos*, that "the Cosmos [is] all there is, all there was, and all there will ever be."[16]

What does Scripture say on this matter?
Read Genesis 1:26–31

Psalm 8:3–4, 5–9

Psalm 144:3–4

Psalm 148

An Alternative Way to Understand Early Genesis, Especially Genesis 1

To begin with, we can say that Genesis was written *for* us, but not *to* us. It was written to an ancient people; therefore, to comprehend it we must comprehend *their* language and *their* culture. We err when we assume that Genesis 1 is easy to apply to our time; i.e., "God said it, I believe it, and that settles it." Also, we need to understand that the culture of the people of Israel had much more in common with other ancient cultures than with ours.

Based on our reading of the publications of Old Testament scholars,[18] the central theme of Genesis 1 appears to be the following: in what can be called a beautiful love poem, God says in effect, "You fear darkness, water, sea monsters, etc., but *every* aspect of my creation is good and functions for your benefit. Fear only me. I created time (day one); the weather (day two); food/plants that multiply (day three); celestial bodies that mark time (day four); fish and birds that multiply (day five); other animals that multiply (day six); and man, formed in my own image (day six)." Throughout Genesis 1 the theme is how each part of creation glorifies the Creator and was ordered for the benefit of humankind—the point is neither *how* nor *when* each was created.

Professor Walton states in the introduction to his book titled *The Lost World of Adam and Eve: Genesis 2–3 and the Human Origins Debate,*

> I will not give very much attention to the legitimacy of the scientific claims. [Rather] I will be conducting a close reading of the Bible as an ancient document *and* as Scripture to explore the claims it makes. The focus will be Genesis, but I will bring the full canon under consideration. I will not be trying to isolate *the* right answer or interpretation but will attempt to show that there are faithful readings of Scripture that … find support in the text and are compatible with what we find in the context of the ancient Near East as well as with some of the more recent scientific discoveries. At the same time, the broad spectrum of core theology

is retained: the authority of Scripture, God's intimate and active role as Creator … that material creation was ex nihilo, that we have all been created by God, and that there was a point in time when sin entered the world, therefore necessitating salvation.

We are not compelled to bring the Bible into conformity either with its cultural context or with modern science, but if an interpretation of Genesis … coincides with what we find as characteristic of the ancient world or with what seem to be sound scientific conclusions, all the better.[19]

And this he does with remarkable clarity and insight!

Take careful notice of what we know to be true, although it has not been stated in so many words: *God made the Earth and universe knowable to humankind.* All of creation follows the laws of mathematics, physics, thermodynamics, optics, etc., so that by studying this creation we can grow in our understanding of the Creator and glorify him in the process. For us as scientists, this is the best part. God didn't keep us in the dark; he reveals his creative truth to us so that we can understand the depth of his plans for humanity and the rest of his magnificent creation, and partner with him as stewards of it all. This is profound!

Questions for Lesson Five

1. Was Noah's flood global in scope?

2. Some people take Genesis 2:5 literally and believe that there had been no rain on the Earth before God created Adam. What do you think?

3. Was there death before the fall?
   Read Romans 5:14

   1 Corinthians 15:21

4. Whom did Cain fear?
   Read Genesis 4:14–16

5. Did hominids such as Neanderthals have souls?

6. What can science teach us about when the Neanderthals lived?

7. Who were the Nephilim?
   Read Genesis 6:1–5

   Numbers 13:33

   Deuteronomy 2:10–11

Why This Really Matters

"Maybe we should revisit the jelly doughnut theory..."

As Dr. Winter alluded (as quoted in Lesson 3), there is a very good chance that the sons and daughters of the church, if raised in a context of "young Earth Christianity," will have their faith needlessly and inevitably shaken in college when confronted with the scientific fact of an old Earth or the evidence for evolution. For example, when I (FDH) taught Freshman Chemistry at Occidental College, my students would calculate the age of a rock based on its isotope data (as described in Lesson 2). This type of problem appears in basically all introductory chemistry textbooks. During the ensuing in-class discussion, I would announce that I would be happy to meet one-on-one with anyone whose faith had been shaken by this calculation. Few professors would be so concerned.

People who insist on a young Earth are not only deterring scientifically-minded people from coming to faith but are also throwing away one of the most persuasive arguments for the existence of a Creator God. Try as they might—and they do—scientists have not been able to propose a rational alternative to the Big Bang Theory. The best science we have tells us that the universe had a beginning and that it started *from nothing* at a known point in space. That's powerful!

We can think of two ways in which you can promote the acceptance of mainstream science in your own Christian realm of church and school. First, even if you don't have children in grades K–12, it is essential that you push your Christian school board to hire teachers who accept the concept of an old Earth and the suggestion that God may well have used evolutionary processes and long time periods to create the Earth. Second, go out of your way to support church members who are scientists. These individuals are sometimes criticized, marginalized, or viewed with suspicion for their views. For example, we knew a chemical engineer who volunteered to teach Sunday school at her church. Shortly thereafter she was told she could not talk to her class about dinosaurs. That was the end of her Sunday school teaching.

Questions for Lesson Six

1. In your estimation, can Christians legitimately accept the possibility that the Creator God may have used evolutionary processes to create life on Earth over millions of years? Why or why not?

2. Some scientists have suggested that there may be an infinite number of universes, the implication being that the unique properties of *this* universe, which supports life, are actually random. What is your response to this suggestion?

3. What do Christians lose if they decide to "write off" science?

Topics for Further Study and Discussion

A surprising amount of what we deal with and vote on in America today involves science, at least at some level. As an example, to help you look at things from that perspective, we now suggest the topic of climate change for further study and discussion. What difference does our faith make in how we respond to the threat of climate change?

Much has been made of how people's opinions about important aspects of climate change tend to correlate with their political party in America. This should, of course, be the case if we are talking about what we should do about climate change— that is a political question, and it is natural that different political parties would propose differing solutions to such an important problem. But there are also differing opinions about the scientific facts of climate change, which we as scientists find very unfortunate. What's going on here?

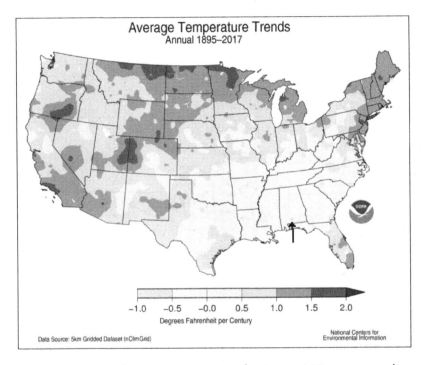

Fig.10: Measured temperature trends since 1895, expressed as changes in temperature per century (National Centers for Environmental Information, National Oceanic and Atmospheric Administration (NOAA), 2018).

While polling indicates that differing opinions on climate change often correlate with political party affiliation in America, there are other important variables that also correlate with views on climate change, such as where people live. For example, according to a 2016 study by the Yale Program on Climate Change Communication,[24] the lowest percentages of registered Democrats who agree that climate change is happening now (66-70%) are those who live in Alabama and Mississippi. Why do 1/3 of registered Democrats from these two states disagree that climate change is currently happening? Before you start to think any negative thoughts about Alabamians and Mississippians, take a look at Figure 10, which shows the total temperature changes observed across the contiguous United States since 1895.

From this map we see an important reason why people in America's "deep south" are more likely to believe that climate change is not happening yet: *in the "deep south," climate change hasn't happened yet*, at least not in terms of measurable changes in average temperatures on land. There is even one part of southern Alabama that has a slight cooling trend over the last 130 years! (The arrow points to a small gray spot. It is the only place in the country, and one of the few places worldwide, where this is true.)

Almost everywhere else in America, in Florida, the Northeast, the Midwest, the West, and the West Coast, temperatures have already risen a measurable amount—more than 1.5 °F in some places—and in these places, people are much more likely to agree that the climate is changing. So what we can see is that we are less likely to dismiss what scientists are saying about the climate if our own lived experience agrees with their conclusions. Another way of looking at this is to ask, if public opinion correlates with local climate change, can people somehow sense temperature changes of only 0.5 to 1.5 °F per century, when they live through much larger temperature swings every day and every season? But even small changes in average temperatures may cause noticeable effects. For example, gardeners—except those in the "deep south"—may notice their flowers blooming earlier than they used to. Farmers may notice changes in harvest times. Westerners can hardly overlook the fact that the fire season is longer and more intense than it used to be. Is climate change causing these differences?

So, here are the facts about climate change: as you can see from the map in Figure 10, most of the United States, and indeed the vast majority of places on earth, have recorded average temperature increases in the last century. The temperature increases on land have generally been larger than those over the oceans, and the temperature increases in the Arctic have been the largest of all. Most of this increase has taken place since about 1970. At the same time, by burning vast quantities of fossil fuels in power plants and for transportation, people have increased the level of greenhouse gases in the atmosphere, which trap some of the heat radiating off of the earth's surface. For example, the concentration of CO_2 (carbon dioxide, a very important greenhouse gas) has increased from 280 to over 400 ppm (parts per million) since the industrial revolution began, with much of this increase *also* taking place in the last 50 years. The heat-trapping nature of greenhouse gases has been known for over a century. None of this is opinion; the last statement is history.

Now, if we increase the concentrations of heat-trapping gases in the atmosphere, what is likely to happen? The laws of physics tell us that the total incoming and outgoing energy flow to a planet (any planet!) must be equal, or the temperature of that planet will change to reflect the imbalance. The incoming energy (from the sun) is nearly constant, so if the outgoing energy flow is being cut down by greenhouse gases, the planetary temperature will rise. The only question is, "How much?" This is the question that climate scientists are trying to answer. It is a fiendishly difficult question, because our planet is divinely complex.

Some of this complexity has to do with the oceans, which currently absorb almost half of the CO_2 we add to the atmosphere. Unfortunately, the ability of the oceans to absorb CO_2 will decline as they get warmer, so the oceans may help us less and less in the future. In addition, as more CO_2 has dissolved into the ocean it has already become measurably more acidic, and at some point this acidity will spell the end of shellfish, coral reefs, and any other organism that builds itself out of calcium carbonate, a substance that is slowly destroyed by dilute acid.

Other complexity involves how plants will respond to higher CO_2 in the atmosphere. On the one hand, plants pull CO_2 out of the air using photosynthesis, using the carbon to grow and build trunks, leaves, and stems, so higher CO_2 in the atmosphere can promote faster plant growth. On the other hand, if climate change is raising the temperature and changing rainfall patterns, large-scale plant die-offs may occur due to the stress of heat and drought, as the optimal climate zone for a particular species of plant moves away from the equator over time. People also seem to have a propensity for cutting down forests. In such an environment, it becomes difficult to determine whether CO_2 uptake by plants will increase or decrease in the future.

One of the biggest categories of climate complexity is the response of water. Warmer temperatures will cause more water to evaporate from oceans, rivers, lakes, and soils, and this evaporated water is also a very important greenhouse gas that, like CO_2, traps heat. However, more evaporated water could also cause clouds to become more widespread globally. Depending on the height and location at which these clouds form, their ability to reflect light and cause cooling will, sometimes, outrun the warming effect of the increased water vapor. The amount of clouds is also influenced by the amount of tiny aerosol particles in the atmosphere, and people (and power plants) have a large effect on the amount of these particles that are present.

Perhaps the largest complexity of all is that people may or may not make a concerted effort to reduce their CO_2 emissions in the future. Our future actions will depend on the political climate, on the development of technology, on economics, on social trends, and, we believe, on the willingness of people of faith to take the lead in protecting the environment.

In the past, environmental problems were often solved by identifying the polluter causing the problem, and then either shutting down the polluter or cleaning up the polluting process. For example, we've eliminated certain refrigerant gases that were causing the ozone hole. We now have catalytic converters on our cars to vastly reduce the amount of smog in U.S. cities. With climate change and CO_2 emissions, however, when we point the finger at the polluter, we realize that we are pointing at ourselves. Our vehicles, our power plants that generate our electricity, our products that we buy—all of these things have contributed and are contributing to climate change. If we want to do something about climate change, we realize, we need to do something ourselves, in addition to any other activism or political action we might take. On some level, we need to change how we live, because how we live is causing a problem.

Realizing that I am causing a problem and changing how I live, in some way, to lessen that problem—this is a definition of repentance. This is why we believe that people of faith need to take the lead in doing something about climate change. People of faith are, or should be, experts in the art of repentance. If we don't model repentance and change in the face of climate change, and the threat it represents to the diversity and health of God's creation, there will not likely be others willing to repent and change.

Questions for Lesson Seven

1. Few deny the fact that the earth is undergoing significant climate change. However, some would argue that this has nothing to do with humankind. What do you think?

   It is naïve and presumptuous to believe that humanity's role in global climate change can be dismissed without seeking help from scientists actively researching the matter.

   Suggested helpful sources:

   - Ongoing reports by the International Governmental Panel on Climate Change (IPCC)

   - A Creation Stewardship Task Force, dealing with climate change and related matters, published in full in the Christian Reformed Church (CRC) 2012 Agenda for Synod, along with its recommendations. This thorough, thoughtful piece was assembled by 11 authors, including some of the best minds in the CRC denomination.

   - This report is available as appendix C of the document at https://www.crcna.org/sites/default/files/2012_agenda.pdf .[22]

   - Searching "Global climate change" will result in many sites summarizing the scientific consensus, which is that it is 95% likely that humans are the cause of climate change. We recommend https://climate.nasa.gov/evidence/ and the IPCC summary report at http://www.ipcc.ch/pdf/assessment-report/ar5/syr/AR5_SYR_FINAL_SPM.pdf .

2. What are greenhouse gases? Why are they given that name?

3. So why is this a problem?

4. Some insist that fossil fuels, especially coal, should be left in the ground. Others argue that coal is our cheapest and most abundant fuel, and we cannot afford *not* to continue to mine and burn it. What do you think?

5. Assuming that new "clean" power plants replace the old polluters, is there a place for fossil fuels? All the fossil fuels produce CO_2, with coal being the worst, then petroleum, then natural gas. Given that it is the primary cause of global climate change, can anything be done to keep CO_2 from becoming airborne?

6. Hasn't the earth warmed and cooled repeatedly over the millions of years of its existence? Why the concern over the current warming pattern?

7. We highly recommend *The Sixth Extinction*, Elizabeth Kolbert, Picador Books, 2014.

8. "The Clean Energy Scam. Hyped as an eco-friendly fuel, ethanol increases global warming, destroys forests and inflates food prices. So why are we subsidizing it?" See article by Michael Grunwald, *Time*, April 7, 2008, pp. 39–45, at http://content.time.com/time/magazine/article/0,9171,1725975,00.html .

9. Also see https://www.afdc.energy.gov/fuels/ethanol_fuel_basics.html .

More Topics for Further Discussion

11. THOU SHALT INSTALL SOLAR PANELS

12. THOU SHALT SET THINE THERMOSTAT TO 68 DEGREES

13. THOU SHALT DRIVE A PRIUS

1. So what is the take-home picture regarding global climate change?

2. Okay, I'm convinced that global climate change is a serious problem. What can I do to help?

Notes

1. Figures 1, 2, 3: http://pubs.usgs.gov/publications/text/historical. html#anchor4833509 .
2. Figure 4. Plate tectonics—Wikipedia. See Floating continents, Plate tectonic theory, and Explanation of magnetic striping.
3. Figure 5 taken from Wikipedia, accessed 2017, page URL: https:// commons.wikimedia.org/wiki/File%3AGeomagnetic_axial_dipole_ strength.svg .

   File URL: https://upload.wikimedia.org/wikipedia/commons/a/ a4/Geomagnetic_axial_dipole_strength.svg .

   Attribution: By Cavit (Own work) [CC BY 4.0 (http:// creativecommons.org/licenses/by/4.0)], via Wikimedia Commons.

   For further discussion and a longer time series of the Earth's magnetic field strength, as estimated from archaeological materials, see also Davis A. Young, *Christianity and the Age of the Earth*, Zondervan, Grand Rapids (1982), pp. 117–124.

   For the creationist viewpoint, see http://creation.com/the-earths- magnetic-field-evidence-that-the-earth-is-young . Note that this theory includes the idea that the Earth was created out of 100% water that was all magnetically aligned, and that most of the water was later changed into rocks and minerals by divine action.
4. Figure 6 is taken from NOAA's National Center for Environmental Information mapping website, https://maps.ngdc.noaa.gov/viewers/ historical_declination/ , accessed 2017.
5. Data from Friedlander, J. W. Kennedy, J. M. Miller, *Nuclear and Radiochemistry*, 2nd ed., John Wiley and Sons, New York (1949), Appendix E, Table of Nuclides, pp. 560, 561, and 564.
6. Figure 7 graph constructed from information available at http://www. periodictable.com/Properties/A/StableIsotopes.html .

7. Davis A. Young, *Christianity and the Age of the Earth*, Zondervan, Grand Rapids (1982), pp. 99–116. Used with permission.

8. Searching for information about the Big Bang Theory is more difficult since the popular TV show came out with the same name, but we recommend the websites https://www.space.com/25126-big-bang-theory.html and https://science.nasa.gov/astrophysics/focus-areas/what-powered-the-big-bang .

9. The 1906 San Francisco earthquake was estimated to have been 7.8 on this scale.

10. A search of "Oklahoma fracking earthquakes" will quickly turn up lots of interesting stories on the increase in small and medium earthquakes since companies started injecting fracking wastewater deep underground. We recommend https://www.marketwatch.com/story/oil-has-made-this-state-the-man-made-earthquake-capital-of-the-world-2016-03-15 .

11. Mission Frontiers, Jan–Feb.(2003), pp. 14–15.

12. William Henry Green, "Primeval Chronology", published in Bibleotheca Sacre, April 1890, pp. 285–303.

13. Davis A. Young, Ralph F. Stearley, *The Bible, Rocks and Time*, InterVarsity Press (2008). pp. 161–162, 396–404, and 430–443. Used with permission.

14. Reference 13, p. 238.

15. http://creation.com/the-biblical-origins-of-science-review-of-stark-for-the-glory-of-god .

16. *When God and Science Meet: Surprising Discoveries of Agreement*, National Association of Evangelicals, 2015, pp. 26, 28. Bulk quantities of this helpful booklet, written by 13 noteworthy authors, are available for a nominal fee plus shipping and handling through the American Scientific Association's (ASA's) website at http://network.asa3.org/general/shop.asp .

17. Melvin Calvin, *"Chemical Evolution. Molecular Evolution towards the Origin of Living Systems on the Earth and Elsewhere*, Oxford University Press, New York, 1969, p. 258.

18. By far the most helpful book regarding Genesis 1 is John H. Walton, *The Lost World of Genesis One*, InterVarsity Press, 2009. Dr. Walton is Professor of Old Testament at Wheaton College.

19. John H. Walton, *The Lost World of Adam and Eve: Genesis 2–3 and the Human Origins Debate*, IVP Academic (2015), pp. 13–14.

20. Gregg Davidson, "Genetics, the Nephilim, and the Historicity of Adam," *Perspectives on Science and Christian Faith*, 67, pp. 24–34. Used with permission. Link to the article: http://www.asa3.org/ASA/PSCF/2015/PSCF3-15Davidson.pdf .

21. J. A. McIntyre, "We Won," *Perspectives on Science and Christian Faith*, 51, 144–145 (Sept. 1999) and "Evolution's Fatal Flaw," Ibid., 162–169. Used with permission.

22. Franklin P. De Haan, "It's Time to Seek Other Seas," *The Banner*, CRC Publications, Grand Rapids, Michigan, December 2016, p. 8. Used with permission.

23. A Creation Stewardship Task Force Report, Agenda, Christian Reformed Church Synod 2012, pp. 287–407. https://www.crcna.org/sites/default/files/2012_agenda.pdf .

24. Elizabeth Kolbert, *The Sixth Extinction*, Picador Books, Henry Holt and Company, LLC (2014), p. 161.

Answers and Comments
for Discussion Questions

Lesson One
The Age of the Earth: Continental Drift

1. **Is the tectonic plate map, Figure 3, an indicator of Earth's major earthquake fault lines?**

    Yes and no. Clearly, some of them, like the San Andreas fault, are predictable from Figure 3. However, there have been major earthquakes that follow faults that are not located along the edges of tectonic plates. For example, in the early 19th century, in 1811–1812, five quakes of an estimated magnitude of 8.0 or higher occurred near New Madrid, Missouri. (The numbers use the Richter Scale, which is logarithmic; i.e., an increase of 1.0 is actually ten times greater.) These quakes are the largest recorded in the contiguous states,[9] so strong they rang church bells in Boston, over 1,000 miles away! They also so changed the contour of the land around New Madrid that it took weeks for the Mississippi River to find a new route to the Gulf of Mexico.

2. **If new solidified magma continues to be formed along the Middle Atlantic Ridge—i.e., the Americas are moving away from Europe and Africa—why is the Earth not increasing in size?**

This is being balanced by instances in which a tectonic plate is wedging itself under another plate. For example, the Nazea plate in the eastern South Pacific is pushing the western part of the South American plate upward, thus forming and growing the Andes Mountains.

As an example close to home, we in Southern California experienced a 6.5–6.7 earthquake in February 1971. After just 12 seconds of shaking, all the hills bordering Los Angeles's San Fernando Valley on the north were 3 feet higher. The upward thrust of this rather modest quake threw sandbags (anchoring a tarp over a swimming pool) onto the roof of a house. Unless you have experienced this, you can't imagine the forces involved. And this involved a modest earthquake along a fault that was barely known and not considered a concern. However, because the San Andreas fault bends in Southern California and hasn't moved since 1857, other fissures break when the pressure builds sufficiently.

3. **Are earthquakes the result of the fall of humanity (Genesis 3)? In other words, is it likely that earthquakes began with Adam?**

   Given the property damage and tragic loss of life in some instances, we have a tendency to ascribe these calamities to humankind's fall through Adam, but the evidence suggests that God was building mountain ranges and moving continents long before Eden.

4. **Is there such a thing as a human-caused earthquake?**

   As a matter of fact, there is.[10] When fracking is used to free underground oil and natural gas from its subterranean locations, the resulting liquid that rises to the surface is a mixture of the desired product—shale oil or natural gas—and water containing dissolved salts, plus some of the original mixture of water and organic compounds used to fracture the rocky layer in the first place. This waste mixture is put back into the Earth through disposal wells, at a depth of up to 2 miles, hopefully well below freshwater aquifers.

The problem occurs when the wastewater seeps into unknown faults, counteracting the friction keeping the fault inactive and thus resulting in fault slippage, i.e., earthquakes.

Take Oklahoma as a case in point. There are more than 3,000 disposal wells, into which over 20 billion gallons of wastewater have been delivered in the last 7 years to the deep Arbuckle layer. The result is striking: before 2009 the state had fewer than 2 earthquakes per year measuring 3 or greater on the Richter scale. In 2015 there were 907, with the largest ever, in Pawnee, measuring 5.8 (September 3, 2015).

The solution is obvious: decrease the volume of injected wastewater. Neighboring Kansas did this and experienced a 60% drop in earthquakes from the previous year. However, when oil prices are low, the Oklahoma oil industry claims it cannot afford to deal with the waste in any other manner— as through reuse, purification, or storage.

5. What is a tsunami? Are these a product of the fall?

A tsunami is basically the displacement of a very large volume of water, usually produced by an earthquake, where tectonic plates overlapping each other give way, with the submersed top plate rising, pushing the ocean upward and producing a broad wave that, when it approaches the shore, increases in magnitude. Landslides, volcanic eruptions, and the calving of glaciers are also known to produce tsunamis. All are natural occurrences and not results of the fall. For reference, see for example http://itic.ioc-unesco.org/index.php?option=com_content&view=article&id=116 2:what-is-a-tsunami&catid=1340&Itemid=2056 .

Lesson Two
The Age of the Earth: Radioactive Decay

1. **If one atom has 80 protons and another has 81 protons, are these different elements or different isotopes?**

   The number of protons in the nucleus determines what type of element an atom is. So these two atoms are different elements. Isotopes have the same number of protons but different numbers of neutrons.

2. **Despite the essential role of trees/forests in removing atmospheric CO_2, what are some factors responsible for continued deforestation in various parts of the Earth?**

   - Ignorance of the process.
   - Pressure from corporations to produce beef, soy, palm oil, and wood products. (from *Chemistry and Engineering News*, 2016)
   - Poverty.
   - Clear-cutting for farming, due to a lack of fertilizers and understanding of crop rotation.

3. **If you were a landholder in Mexico, would clear-cutting your forest and planting avocado trees constitute an effective response to the current huge demand emanating from China for that fruit? Why or why not?**
    We would be tempted, given the demand and the consistent high price. For us as Earth-keepers, the environmentally responsible action would be to ascertain how avocado trees compare to your current trees in removing CO_2 from the atmosphere. Deforestation has other serious effects, especially in tropic zones. See Lesson 7, question 6.

4. **Why is the age of the oldest rock not synonymous with the age of the Earth?**
    Astrogeologists believe that the energy produced through nuclear reactions was sufficient to keep the early Earth in liquid form. Only when these processes lessened did the Earth cool sufficiently that solid rocks—granite, etc.— were formed at the surface, thus trapping U atoms within the crystal lattice. This means that the Earth is older than the oldest rock.

5. **Why do this book's authors suggest 50,000 years as a practical limit to C-14 dating?**
    Following the example on the top of page 24, 50,000 years is roughly 9 half-lives, i.e., $1/2^9 = 1/512$, which means that you are working with only 0.2 % of the C-14 originally there, which was only a tiny fraction of the C-12 initially! Current instrumentation can "see" one C-14 in 10^{12} C-12 atoms. That's 1 followed by 12 zeros—1,000,000,000,000, or one of a trillion! After 9+ half-lives you are usually pushing these limits.

6. For those with an algebra/high school chemistry background, note that Figure 8 can also be expressed in straight line form. Since radioactive decay is a first-order process, i.e., depends only on the number of radioactive atoms present, it follows the equation

$$\frac{-dN}{dt} = \text{Rate of decay} = kN$$

where k is the first-order rate constant and N is the number of radioactive atoms. Using calculus, this equation becomes

$$\frac{-kt}{2.3} = \log \frac{N_t}{N_0} \qquad (1)$$

where t is the time span of the decay, N_0 the original number of radioactive atoms at t = 0, and N_t the number remaining at the end of the time interval. It follows that

$$\text{when } t = t_{1/2}, N_t = N_0 / 2$$
and thus
$$k = 0.693 / t_{1/2} \qquad (2)$$

Problem: If a rock contains 0.130 mg of Pb-206 for every 1.0 mg of U-238, how old is the rock? The half-life of U-238 is 4.51 x 10^9 years. What assumption must you make?

Solution:

Combining (1) and (2) by eliminating k and rearranging, we have

$$\frac{-0.693\,t}{t_{1/2}\,2.30} = \log\frac{N_t}{N_0}$$

or

$$t = \frac{-2.30\,t_{1/2}}{0.693}\log\frac{N_t}{N_0}$$

Assume that all the Pb–206 came after the rock had crystallized.

$$0.130 \text{ mg Pb–206 } (238/206) = 0.150 \text{ mg U-238}$$

Therefore, the original sample had

$$1.0 \text{ mg} + 0.150 \text{ mg} = 1.15 \text{ mg U-238} = N_0$$

Therefore

$$t = \frac{-2.30\,(4.5 \times 10^9 \text{ yr})}{0.693}\log\frac{1.0}{1.15}$$

$$= 9 \times 10^8 \text{ years}$$

7. **For those interested in science, predict the mode of decay of $_{78}Pt^{186}$. The Periodic Table records the atomic weight of platinum as 195.08, which is a weighted average of six stable isotopes.**

    Since N/Z is $108/78 < 1.5$ is well below that for the stable isotopes of Platinum, electron capture (EC), which increases N/Z, is predicted.

Lesson Three
The Age of the Universe: The Big Bang Theory

1. **When did God create the universe?**

   Genesis 1 does not speak to this, other than to say "In the beginning."

2. **How did God create the universe?**

   Genesis 1 is not an attempt by God to explain the science behind creation to the Israelites or to us. Nor does he do this anywhere else in Scripture.

3. **What did ancient/biblical peoples fear?**

   Read Job 3:8

   Job 7:12

   Psalm 148:7

   Isaiah 27:1

   Isaiah 30:7

   Isaiah 51:9

   They feared chaos, darkness, water, and sea monsters.

4. **How did ancient/biblical people view the Earth?**

   Read Genesis 7:11

   Psalm 24:1–2

   Psalm 78:23

   Psalm 104:5

   Psalm 148:4

   Proverbs 8:27–28

   Isaiah 24:18b

   Isaiah 40:22

The ancients pictured the Earth as basically flat, with hills and mountains and with water below and water above, as shown in this picture (taken from http://barrybandstra.com).

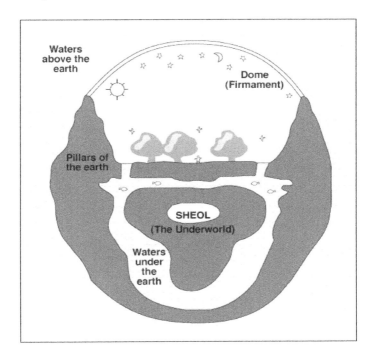

God doesn't correct that view in Genesis 1:6–8. Nor does he do this in the description of the beginnings of the flood in Genesis 7:11.

5. **Where did God dwell?**
   Read Psalm 104:3
   Amos 9:6

This is more difficult to ascertain. The verses suggest that the ancients envisioned God as dwelling somewhere above the waters above the sky.

6. Were the days of creation 24-hour days as we know them?

The obvious answer, based on the creation of time being mentioned before that of the sun, moon, and stars, is no. And the scientific evidence we have bears this out.

As you see by our basic, limited discussion of the scientific approaches to determine the age of the Earth (and the universe), the answer is to consider the repetitive phrase "There was evening and there was morning" of Genesis 1 as a cadence to God's love poem to humankind rather than as a scientific statement.

7. Does God speak through creation, or only through the Bible?

Read Psalm 19:1
Psalm 111:2
Psalm 145
Psalm 147
Psalm 148
Colossians 1:15–17

All through Scripture we are told that God speaks to us through his creation, as well as through the Bible. This was clear to our church fathers. Already in Article 2 of the Belgic Confession, adopted in 1618 along with the Heidelberg Catechism and the Canons of Dort as doctrinal standards for those of the Reformed faith, we read:

We know him by two means:

First, by the creation, preservation and government
       of the universe,
Since that universe is before our eyes
Like a beautiful book
      In which all creatures,
      Great and small
      Are as letters
      To make us ponder
      The invisible things of God:
            His eternal power
            And his divinity,
      As the apostle Paul says in Romans 1:20.
      All these things are enough to convict men
      And to leave them without excuse.

Second, he makes himself known to us more openly
By his holy and divine Word,
As much as we need in this life,
For his glory
And for the salvation of his own.

Lesson Four
Where Does the Idea of a Young Earth and Universe Come From?

1. What is "flood geology"?

Since the 1930s the idea that Noah's flood alone produced the stratigraphy of the Earth has been promoted by a few people who also believe in a young Earth. They go on to insist that the "fossil record" as published is false or even a lie, i.e., "a fiction conceived by atheists bent on proving preconceived notions of evolution." However, those who founded the science of biostratigraphy were actively at work well before Darwin's *The Origin of Species* was published "and were in fact indifferent or hostile to the concept of organic evolution."[14]

2. **Why was Ussher's 1658 estimate of the age of the universe generally accepted for 150 years?**
    As far as the motion of the planets is concerned, in 1658 the universe appeared to have been running indefinitely from the distant past. The genealogies in Genesis seemed like a good place to look to answer this question. There really wasn't any scientific data available.

3. **The scientific evidence in support of an ancient Earth and universe slowly accumulates, becoming stronger with each passing year. According to Gallup polls, 65–70% of weekly church-going Christians believe that God created humans in their present form within the last 10,000 years, and this percentage has held steady for at least 35 years. Why do you think this is so?**
    See the Davis and Stearley quote at the end of Lesson 4 for several possible reasons.

4. **Many assume that science and religion have always disagreed. Is this accurate?**
    Hardly. In his book *For the Glory of God* Rodney Stark studied scholar scientists of the 1543–1680 era, i.e., the beginning of the scientific period.[15] Of his top 52, he

categorized 50 as Christians, evenly divided between Protestants and Catholics, with 30 of these characterized as "devout"; the other two he saw as a skeptic and a pantheist.

As John Ortberg states, "The rise of science required a worldview that posited a world that is orderly and will reward rational investigation. That worldview arose from faith in an all-powerful, rational God."[16] In *Chemical Evolution* the Nobel Prize-winning biochemist Melvin Calvin said, "This monotheistic view seems to be the historical foundation for modern science." [17]

5. **Why do some scientists push the idea that given the immensity of the universe humankind is insignificant? John Ortberg quotes astronomer Carl Sagan, who wrote that the Earth is "an insignificant planet of a humdrum star lost in a galaxy tucked away in some forgotten corner of a universe in which there are far more galaxies than people." Sagan also said, when introducing his TV program titled *The Cosmos,* that "the Cosmos [is] all there is, all there was, and all there will ever be."[16]**
    What does Scripture say on this matter?
    Read Genesis 1:26–31
    Psalm 8:3–4, 5–9
    Psalm 144:3–4
    Psalm 148

Some scientists take pleasure in denigrating the biblical idea that humans have God-given dignity and value. Nor are they willing to accept that the Big Bang Theory cries out for a Creator.

The Bible, in Psalms 8 and 144, agrees with the premise that humankind doesn't amount to much in comparison to the magnitude of the universe. However, Genesis 1:26–31, Psalm 8:5–9, and other passages support the notions of humanity's unique place in creation and our role as Earth-keepers.

Lesson Five
An Alternative Way to Understand Early Genesis, Especially Genesis 1

1. Was Noah's flood global in scope?

A cursory reading of Genesis 7 would seem to support this idea. However, it makes more sense to understand this as a local flood covering the portion of the world known to the writer.

Why? Geologists have found no evidence for a worldwide flood. And there is literally not enough water on the planet and in the atmosphere for such a worldwide catastrophe. Other verses in Genesis suggest that we must be careful with the way we construe the word "all." Genesis 41:48 says, for example, that "Joseph collected all the food produced." This cannot be taken literally, since the Egyptians ate some of it. In addition, Genesis 41:57 states that "all the countries came to Egypt to buy grain from Joseph, because the famine was severe in all the world." As the NIV footnote clarifies, this refers to the "known world from the writer's perspective (the middle East)."

2. **Some people take Genesis 2:5 literally and believe that there had been no rain on the Earth before God created Adam. What do you think?**

Given what we know, this isn't very plausible. The NIV Study Bible (1985) is helpful; it states "or land" for "earth," thus rendering an alternative reading "for the LORD God had not sent rain on the land," as would be expected in an extremely arid region.

3. **Was there death before the fall?**

Read Romans 5:14
1 Corinthians 15:21

Again, given what we know concerning the age of the Earth, the idea that no one or nothing had died before the fall is not remotely realistic. These passages refer to spiritual, not physical death.

4. **Whom did Cain fear?**

Read Genesis 4:14–16

Based on a cursory reading of Genesis, it would appear that early humanity consisted of Adam, Eve, and Cain, now that Abel had been killed. Since no mention of Abel's genealogy is mentioned, it would follow that he died childless. Seth was born after this sad event.

A possible way to explain Cain's fear comes from science. We now know that hominids distinct from *Homo sapiens*—the Neanderthals—predated modern humans by over 100,000 years and coexisted with *Homo sapiens* for thousands of years before they became extinct. And we know a lot about them. The remains of more than 5,000 hominids have been unearthed, including a number of complete skeletons. We also know from DNA analysis that interbreeding occurred between *Homo sapiens* and Neanderthals.

Genesis 6 indicates that there were other hominids contemporary with Adam and Eve's family. In one of his articles Gregg Davidson posits:

1. Adam and Eve were naturally born hominids selected by God from a large group.
2. Selection included endowing with souls, making them spiritually, relationally, and cognitively distinct from their hominid relatives and neighbors. This included their progeny as well.
3. After being cast out of Eden, forbidden interbreeding occurred between their offspring and contemporaneous hominids, thus producing the genetic variation we see today.[19]

4. **Did hominids such as Neanderthals have souls?**
   Davidson suggests that they demonstrated "soulish" behavior, e.g., "loyalty, affection (they decorated their dead before burial), pleasure, excitement, curiosity, sadness, and a measure of self-awareness." It follows that Cain could well have feared these "soulish, human-looking creatures."[20]

5. **What can science teach us about when the Neanderthals lived?**
   A scientist, Sophie Verhayden, was able to date the occupation of the Bruniquel Cave in France by

Neanderthals to 176,500 years ago (The Atlantic, 5/25/16 posting).

6. Who were the Nephilim?

Read Genesis 6:1–5
Numbers 13:33
Deuteronomy 2:10–11

Davidson says that "[i]nterbreeding between the offspring of Adam and Eve with hominids from their ancestral population would not be expected to produce the unusual physical prowess associated with the Nephilim." However, if the timing of Genesis 6 coincides with the period of overlap between humans and Neanderthals, the heavier musculature of the Neanderthals could certainly have resulted in offspring with enhanced strength or unique physical characteristics that made it natural to refer to them by a special name."[20]

Lesson Six
Why This Really Matters

1. In your estimation, can Christians legitimately accept the possibility that the Creator God may have used evolutionary processes to create life on Earth over millions of years? Why or why not?

Many already do. For some, accepting this possibility may involve accepting a different way of interpreting Genesis.

Most of us would agree that God's revelation of himself through his creation must agree with scriptural revelation. After all, all truth is God's truth. God does not contradict himself. Yet many believers continue to insist that Scripture must ultimately be our science guide, following the error of the Catholic church in excommunicating Galileo.

Why so? We suggest that this is partly due to misinterpretation of evolution as being godless. For years the National Academy of Science and others defined evolution as an "unsupervised, impersonal, unpredictable and natural process." However, after being challenged by Christian groups, including the American Scientific Affiliation, they changed their definition of evolution as follows: "The diversity of life on earth is the outcome of evolution; an ~~unsupervised, impersonal,~~ unpredictable and natural process."[21] By dropping those adjectives that imply randomness, evolution, by definition, clearly leaves room for Intelligent Design—for a Creator.[22]

2. **Some scientists have suggested that there may be an infinite number of universes, the implication being that the unique properties of *this* universe, which supports life, are actually random. What is your response to this suggestion?**
    Scientific theories have to be "falsifiable." This means that it must be possible to disprove them. The multiverse theory fails this test, so it can't be characterized as science.

3. **What do Christians lose if they decide to "write off" science?**
    The willingness to ignore scientific data cuts off Christians from one of the two major sources of God's revelation, which is the universe itself. For example,

ignoring scientific data in other fields (two examples: health science, climate science) can result in behavior that is very damaging. So, too, ignoring scientific facts about the Earth and the universe can have disastrous consequences for the children of believers.

Lesson Seven
Topics for Further Study and Discussion

1. **Few deny that the Earth is undergoing significant climate change. However, some would argue that this has nothing to do with humankind. What do you think?**
    It is naïve and presumptuous to believe that humanity's role in global climate change can be dismissed without seeking help from scientists actively researching the matter.

    Suggested helpful sources:

    - Ongoing reports by the International Governmental Panel on Climate Change (IPCC)
    - A Creation Stewardship Task Force, dealing with climate change and related matters, published in full in the Christian Reformed Church (CRC) 2012 Agenda for Synod, along with its recommendations. This thorough, thoughtful piece was assembled by 11 authors, including some of the best minds in the denomination.
    - This report is available as appendix C of the document at https://www.crcna.org/sites/default/files/2012_agenda.pdf .[23]

- Searching "Global climate change" will result in many sites summarizing the scientific consensus, which is that it is 95% likely that humans are the cause of climate change. We recommend https://climate.nasa.gov/evidence/ and the IPCC summary report at http://www.ipcc.ch/pdf/ assessment-report/ar5/syr/AR5_SYR_FINAL_ SPM.pdf .2 .

For a fun illustration, check out "A Timeline of Earth's Average Temperature" since the last ice age glaciation 22,000 years ago. Go to http://xkcd.com/1732/.

The end of this cartoon timeline clearly shows the recent rise in the Earth's temperature, which starts in the early 1900s and accelerates in the last 40–50 years. The change, which correlates with increasing CO_2 emissions, is obviously much more sudden than any of the natural changes over the previous 22,000 years.

2. **What are greenhouse gases? Why are they given that name?**

Primary greenhouse gases are water vapor (H_2O), carbon dioxide (CO_2), methane (CH_4), nitrous oxide (N_2O), and ozone (O_3). They are called that because, like a greenhouse, they let the ultraviolet and visible light from the sun pass through the atmosphere but adsorb and re-emit the thermal infrared radiation emitted by the Earth's surface, thus serving as a blanket. Without these gases the Earth's average temperature would be about 0^0 F rather than the current average of 59^0 F.

3. So why is this a problem?

Of the greenhouse gases, CO_2 is a major concern. Since the advent of the Industrial Revolution , ~ 1750, the atmospheric concentration of CO_2 has increased from 280 parts per million (ppm) to 401 ppm as of September 2016.

Methane, CH_4, absorbs and re-emits infrared (heat) radiation about 100 times more efficiently than CO_2, but it doesn't last as long in the atmosphere as CO_2. (Methane's lifetime in the atmosphere is only 12 years, as compared to CO_2's 30–95 years.) Because methane is present at concentrations of only 2 ppm, it plays a lesser role in global warming, but releases of methane are still harmful.

CO_2, on the other hand, is a major concern. Even though there are natural pathways, such as mixing into the ocean and photosynthesis (see page 59) that remove atmospheric CO_2, the levels of CO_2 continue to increase because of anthropogenic (human) activities, i.e., combustion of carbon-based fuels, principally coal, oil, and natural gas, along with deforestation, soil erosion, and animal agriculture.

4. Some insist that fossil fuels, especially coal, should be left in the ground. Others argue that coal is our cheapest and most abundant fuel and that we cannot afford *not* to continue to mine and burn it. What do you think?

First, the good news:

- The United States has 26% of the world's entire supply of coal, enough for 300 years at current consumption rates. This does not even count

Alaska's coal reserves, which total more than those of the other 49 states combined.

- Technology now exists to convert coal to liquefied natural gas (primarily methane), diesel, gasoline, jet fuel, and methanol (which can be converted to gasoline and other worthwhile products).
- Coal is used in the manufacture of steel, cement, and paper.
- The world's total coal reserves will last for thousands of years at today's consumption rates.

The bad news:

Coal is a "dirty fuel." It contains:

- Mercury, which travels through the air and becomes concentrated in fish. Small amounts can result in heavy-metal poisoning, which is particularly bad for fetuses.
- Polycyclic aromatic hydrocarbons, many of them carcinogenic.
- Radioisotopes Uranium and Thorium.
- Nitrogen and sulfur compounds, which convert to oxides upon combustion and then to acids of nitrogen and sulfur, leading to acid rain.
- Arsenic (1.4-71 ppm) and Selenium (3ppm)

Power stations consume large quantities of water.

In 2010, 13,000 premature deaths and 20,000 heart attacks were attributed to coal combustion in the US. The total cost of health impacts that year were estimated to be over $100 billion.

In China, air pollution from burning coal kills an average of 4,400 people a day.

Back to the good news:
Modern technology has developed filters and precipitators, etc., to remove most of these impurities. These are known as "clean coal" plants.

More bad news:
Unfortunately, most coal-fired plants have not been upgraded. Many municipalities state that they do not have the financial resources to pay for these improvements.

Case in point: Michigan. Throughout the state pregnant women are warned to minimize their consumption of large fish from the Great Lakes, lake trout, and salmon. Being at the top of the aquatic food chain, these fish have high mercury concentrations. Along the west coast of that state, cities like Muskegon, Grand Haven, etc., have not updated their power plants. The known exception is the city of Holland, where a brand new plant burns natural gas, a much cleaner fuel.

However, in February 2018, Michigan's two largest electricity providers announced they will phase out" coal by 2040.

The coal industry lobby has forced the Environmental Protection Agency (EPA) to ignore health issues when judging the costs of energy generation.

The coal industry has a lamentable record when it comes to cleaning up its "mess" after coal mines are played out. Many of West Virginia's mined areas, for example, are ecological disasters.

5. **Assuming that new, "clean" power plants replace the old polluters, is there a place for fossil fuels? All the fossil fuels produce CO_2, with coal being the worst, followed in order by petroleum and natural gas. Given that the burning of fossil fuels constitutes the primary cause of global climate change, can anything be done to keep CO_2 from becoming airborne?**

This is the $64,000 question. Some have suggested sequestration of liquid CO_2 deep in the Earth. Icelandic scientists are currently exploring adding CO_2 back into geothermal vents where, at the vent's elevated temperatures, it reacts with subsurface calcium oxide (CaO) or calcium chloride ($CaCl_2$) to become inert calcium carbonate ($CaCO_3$). This approach is obviously limited to locations with geothermal activity.

Chemists have recently reported the conversion of CO_2 into polymers, including a superior biodegradable plastic. Feasibility depends on efficient means to capture the CO_2, preferably before it is airborne, and transport it to a chemical plant, as well as on the comparable costs of other polymers.

6. **Hasn't the Earth warmed and cooled repeatedly over the millions of years of its existence? Why the concern over the current warming pattern?**

We highly recommend *The Sixth Extinction*, Elizabeth Kolbert, Picador Books, 2014.

Since most species thrive in specific temperature ranges, their survival depends on their ability to migrate. During the current warming period, this means moving to cooler regions.

We don't think of trees migrating, but their survival also depends on temperature. In one of the *Sixth Extinction* chapters, Kolbert uses tree migration as an important example of essential species we see as "root-bound." Trees "migrate" by dropping seeds; thus with warming, trees move upslope at varying speeds. In areas under study in Peru, some 1,035 tree species have been identified (compare that to Canada, which has ¼ of the intact forests on the Earth but only 20 tree species). Those doing the Peruvian tree study have found that trees are moving to cooler, higher altitudes at a great variety of speeds, ranging from some not at all to one hyperactive genus, *Schefflera*, at nearly 100 ft/year.

> In its magnitude, the temperature change projected for the coming century is roughly the same as the temperature swings of the ice ages. (If the current emissions trends continue, the Andes are expected to warm by as much as nine degrees.) But if the magnitude of the change is similar, the rate is not, and once again, rate is key. Warming today is taking place at least 10 times faster than it did at the end of the last glaciation, and at the end of all those glaciations that preceded it. To keep up, organisms will have to migrate, or otherwise adapt, at least 10 times more quickly.[24]

Clearly, if humankind does not alleviate global warming, many, many plant and animal species will not survive. Thus the title *The Sixth Extinction* for Kolbert's book, in which she also discusses the fate of a number of animal species. As the précis states, "The sixth extinction is likely to be mankind's most lasting legacy."

7. **See the article by Michael Grunwald, "The Clean Energy Scam. Hyped as an eco-friendly fuel, ethanol increases global warming, destroys forests and inflates food prices. So why are we subsidizing it?" in Time, April 7, 2008, pp. 39–45, at http://content.time.com/time/ magazine/article/0,9171,1725975,00.html .**
Also see https://www.afdc.energy.gov/fuels/ethanol_ fuel_basics.html .

Some 10 years later it is still instructive to visit the points made by Mr. Grunwald.

Based on the carbon content of gasoline (8 carbon atoms/molecule) vs. ethanol (2/molecule), one would expect that a mixture of 90% gasoline and 10% ethanol should produce a lesser quantity of greenhouse gases (CO_2). However, other factors are at play. First, the electricity involved in converting corn to ethanol comes mainly from coal. Second, when you calculate the maximum amount of energy produced by the combustion of a mixture of 90%/10% gasoline/ethanol to that of gasoline alone, you find that adding 10% ethanol decreases it by 7.6%. Thus your MPG have decreased by roughly 10%, and your car is using almost 10% more energy to travel a given distance. (This was verified with my [FDH] 2009 Honda Civic. Back when you could choose between straight gasoline or the 9010 mixture, the average mileage on many cross-country tankfulls dropped from 40 MPG to 37 MPG with the mixture.)

The picture is worse than that. Hundreds of thousands of acres of Brazilian rainforest, the world's best storehouse of carbon, are being converted to soy beans and other crops for ethanol production. In just half of 2007, 750,000 acres were lost (equal to the size of Rhode Island). That's just Brazil. When deforestation is included in the calculations, the effect on greenhouse gas emissions from 10% ethanol addition is an increase of 93% relative to gasoline alone.

The congressional Budget Office in 2010 estimated that the taxpayer cost to reduce gasoline consumption by one gallon was $1.78 for corn ethanol!

Additionally, bioethanol production has had a major impact on grain supplies around the world. Ethanol demand adds anywhere from 75 cents to $1 per bushel to the price of corn and products derived from corn.

The reason Brazilian forests are being replaced by soy bean fields has its origins in the US. Attracted by government subsidies, many American farmers, including those operating mega-farms, switched to growing corn instead of soy beans. As expected, the soy bean price went up, encouraging Brazilians to get into the market.

Will it ever stop? The $6 billion/year Volumetric Ethanol Excise Tax Credit expired in 2011. Yet Congress and the Administration mandated 15 billion gallons of corn ethanol for 2015 and plans to have this up to 36 billion gallons in 2022. Incredible. You see the power of the Corn Ethanol lobby.

There is one ray of sunshine, sugarcane-based ethanol. Because the production of ethanol from sugarcane requires only half the energy of the corn to ethanol process, there is a net drop in CO_2 emissions via this method.

Already in 2007 combined exports of cane-sugar derived ethanol to the US from Jamaica, El Salvador, Trinidad and Tobago, Costa Rica, and Brazil reached 420 million gallons, 98.3% of ethanol imports. Domestic production of ethanol from sugarcane, from Florida, Hawaii, Louisiana, Texas, and California, amounted to 220 million gallons in 2011. As in other cases, the bottom line question must be asked: How much of the sugarcane acreage results from deforestation?

Lesson Eight
More Topics for Further Discussion

1. **So what is the take-home picture regarding global climate change?**

    The Creation Stewardship Task Force Report[23] states the situation clearly.

    Quoting from page 381 of that report:

    Human induced climate change is a matter of urgent and profound concern.

    The Earth's climate is changing, with adverse effects on people, communities and ecosystems.

    •   There is now high confidence in the scientific evidence of human influence on climate as detailed by the Intergovernmental Panel on Climate Change (IPCC) and endorsed by 18 of the world's leading Academies of Science.

- Human activities, especially the burning of coal, oil and natural gas (fossil fuels) are rapidly increasing the concentrations of greenhouse gases (especially carbon dioxide) in the global atmosphere. As a result the global climate is warming, with rising sea levels, changes in rainfall patterns, more floods and droughts, and more intense storms. These have serious social, economic and ecological consequences.

- The harmful effects of climate change far outweigh the beneficial ones:

  - In many arid and semi-arid areas, the quantity and quality of fresh water will continue to decrease.

  - Although agricultural productivity may increase in temperate northern latitudes, it will decrease throughout the tropics and sub-tropics.

  - A greater incidence of diseases, such as malaria, dengue fever and cholera, is expected.

  - Sea-level rise and increased flooding is already displacing people and will eventually affect tens of millions, especially in low-income countries. Some island states are likely to disappear altogether.

  - Important ecosystems, such as coral reefs and forests, will be destroyed or drastically altered, undermining the very foundation of a sustainable world.

2. **Okay, I'm convinced that global climate change is a serious problem. What can I do to help?**

   For openers, support Congressional candidates who believe in humankind's role in global climate change and are dedicated to action. At last count there were 183 members of Congress who denied it! Unbelievable. The League of Conservation Voters lists all candidates' positions on this all-important matter.

   Second, hold a mini-workshop. Encourage each other to meet as small groups, perhaps with your Bible study group, adult Sunday school class, etc., and deal with the question "What can I do as a person, or we as a family or church group or congregation or community, to be more effective as Earth-keepers?" Our friend Dr. David Tan, an expert on global warming, stated, "There may be no 'silver bullet' solution for global warming, but there are silver buckshot." By that he is was suggesting that there are many things we can do, individually and collectively, to decrease our carbon footprint and together help solve the problem.

   Third, broaden your idea list by reading the many recommendations from the 2012 Synodical committee report,[23] pp. 400–406, and a congregational checklist, pp. 395–397.

   Finally, be an Earth-keeper in both prayer and action.

About the Authors

Franklin P. De Haan, currently Carl F. Braun Professor of Chemistry, Emeritus, taught general, inorganic, and physical chemistry at Occidental College, Los Angeles, from 1961 through 1995. His research on the kinetics and mechanisms of electrophilic aromatic substitution reactions was funded by the Research Foundation, ACS-PRF, NSF, NSF-RUI, NSF-REU, and the Dreyfus Foundation (total support over $2M) and resulted in 25 publications, 18 of which included undergraduate authors, 85 in all (including his son David). Among his many awards, he was named California Professor of the Year by the Carnegie Foundation in 1987. He earned an AB (Chemistry, Mathematics) from Calvin College in 1957 and his PhD (Physical and Inorganic Chemistry) from Purdue in 1961. He has been an active member of Bethel Christian Reformed Church, Sun Valley, California, since 1961, serving on various committees and as a deacon, then elder, and of late as Council President. His service for Classis Greater Los Angeles includes its Race Relations, Strategic Planning, and Leadership Teams. He has served on the Home Missions Committee and twice as a Synodical delegate.

David O. De Haan serves as Professor of Chemistry and Biochemistry at the University of San Diego. He joined the USD faculty in 2001. He teaches courses in general, analytical, and environmental chemistry that incorporate active learning techniques (e.g., POGIL, online polling) and open-ended, research-like lab experiences. His research program in lab

101

simulations of aerosol/haze formation by aqueous chemical processes has been continuously funded since 2007 by the NSF's Division of Atmospheric and Geospace Sciences through the RUI program. Sixty undergraduates, seven high school students, and three postdoctoral researchers have been mentored by Professor De Haan in the research lab since 2001, and this work has resulted in 24 publications, 19 of which have included undergraduate co-authors. He was one of the first two recipients of USD's Outstanding Research Mentor Award in 2012, the year this award was inaugurated. He earned his BSc (Chemistry) from Calvin College and his PhD (Analytical and Environmental Chemistry) from the University of Colorado, Boulder. He attends Redemption Church in San Diego, California.

Made in the USA
Monee, IL
04 December 2019